IMPROVING THE MENTAL HEALTH OF YOUR LITTLE ONE

Practicable Steps to Enhancing Mental Balance

JULIAN TIM

Copyright © 2023 by Julian Tim

All rights reserved.

No portion of this book may be reproduced in any form without written permission from the publisher or author, except as permitted by U.S. copyright law.

This distribution is intended to give exact and legitimate data concerning the topic covered. It is sold with the comprehension that neither the creator nor the distributor has taken part in delivering medical administration. While the distributor and writer have involved their earnest attempts in setting up this book, they make no portrayals or guarantees regarding the precision or culmination of the items in this book and explicitly disavow any suggested guarantees of qualification for a specific reason. The counsel and procedures contained thus may not be reasonable for your circumstance. You ought to talk with an expert when suitable. Neither the distributor nor the creator will be at risk for any deficiency of benefit.

TABLE OF CONTENTS

INTRODUCTION

The vast majority comprehend the significance of having a sound body. Many individuals, however, neglect the worth of psychological wellness. Having great psychological well-being can make life more pleasant. It can likewise advance better actual well-being and perseverance. You should deal with both your body and mind to be genuinely sound. Progressively, kids ages 3-12 are battling with tension, despondency, and psychological well-being difficulties. These can be welcomed by many elements, for example, stress at home, disturbances in the public eye, breaks in daily practice, segregation from companions, tormenting or prevalent burdens, and so on, and whenever left neglected, they follow kids into their adolescents and adulthood, causing mental, profound, and social issues that will take their tranquility and bliss.

When psychological issues are recognized in youngsters, it needs early mediation and a steady environment as these assume an urgent part in assisting kids with exploring their emotional

4

wellness challenges and further developing their general prosperity. Notwithstanding, it ought to be noticed that each kid is one of a kind, and emotional well-being requirements might differ starting with one youngster and then onto the next. It's critical to give a protected and strong space for youngsters to communicate their feelings, pay attention to their interests, and look for proficient assistance when required.

In this book, practicable steps to enhancing mental balance in children are clearly explained and this can be a step towards gaining mental freedom for your child.

CHAPTER ONE

THE IDEA OF MENTAL HEALTH

Emotional wellness in youngsters alludes to their profound, mental, and social prosperity. It influences kids' thought processes, feelings, and act, and it likewise decides how they handle pressure, connect with others, and simply decide. Very much like grown-ups, kids can encounter a scope of psychological well-being conditions, including uneasiness, despondency, consideration shortfall/hyperactivity jumble, mental imbalance range jumble and more. It is vital to take note that emotional wellness issues in youngsters can be brought about by a mix of hereditary, natural, ecological, and social elements. These may incorporate the family background of psychological wellness issues, injury, drug misuse, neediness, absence of admittance to medical care, or other unfriendly encounters. Nonetheless, distinguishing psychological wellness issues in kids can be trying since they may not necessarily be able to communicate their feelings and sentiments precisely.

Psychological wellness conditions in Kids

Common psychological wellness conditions in Kids include the following:

1. Nervousness Issues: These incorporate circumstances like summed up uneasiness, social tension problems, fear of abandonment, and explicit fears. Kids with uneasiness issues might encounter exorbitant concern, dread, and anxiety that can slow down their day-to-day exercises and general work.

2. Depression: Kids can likewise encounter wretchedness, which includes diligent sensations of trouble, sadness, loss of interest in exercises, changes in craving or rest examples, weakness, and trouble concentrating. Sadness can fundamentally influence a kid's state of mind, conduct, and capacity to work.

3. Attention-Deficit/Hyperactivity Disorder (ADHD): ADHD is a neurodevelopmental problem portrayed by obliviousness, hyperactivity, and impulsivity. Youngsters with ADHD frequently battle with remaining on track, adhering to directions, and arranging undertakings, and may show hasty ways of behaving.

4. Mental imbalance Range Problem: This is a formative problem described by troubles in friendly cooperation, correspondence, and dreary ways of behaving. Kids with this problem might have difficulties with interactive abilities, language improvement, taking part in creative play, and show monotonous ways of behaving or obsessions.

5. Lead Confusion: Direct turmoil includes constant examples of conduct that disregard the privileges of others and cultural standards. Youngsters with direct turmoil frequently show forceful ways of behaving, experience issues observing guidelines, ignore others' sentiments, and may participate in demonstrations of animosity or savagery.

6. Dietary problems: Dietary issues, for example, anorexia nervosa, bulimia nervosa, or pigging out jumble, can likewise happen in kids. These circumstances include aggravations in eating, ways of behaving, self-perception and disappointment. These may prompt serious physical and mental well-being results.

Reasons for psychological wellness issues in youngsters

There can be different reasons for psychological wellness issues in youngsters. It's essential to take note that emotional well-being issues can emerge from a mix of variables, instead of a solitary reason. Some of the causes are listed below:

1. Hereditary qualities: Youngsters might acquire an inclination to specific psychological well-being conditions, like uneasiness or sadness, from their folks or other relatives.

2. Cerebrum science and construction: Lopsided characteristics in mind synthetic substances (synapses) or anomalies in cerebrum design might add to the improvement of psychological well-being issues.

3. Horrible encounters: Encountering or seeing horrendous mishaps, like maltreatment, disregard, brutality, or mishaps, can essentially affect a kid's psychological prosperity.

4. Natural elements: Unpleasant home conditions, residing in destitution, openness to savagery, or conflicting nurturing practices can expand the gamble of psychological well-being issues.

5. Natural factors: Certain ailments or cerebrum issues, for example, ADHD or chemical imbalance range jumble, can likewise be related to emotional wellness issues in youngsters.

6. Mental variables: Elements like low confidence, unfortunate adapting abilities, trouble in dealing with feelings, or having a pessimistic standpoint can add to the improvement of psychological well-being issues.

7. Social elements: Harassing, social segregation, peer tension, or battles with peer connections can adversely influence a kid's psychological prosperity.

8. Family ancestry: Having a family background of emotional well-being issues can build a kid's weakness to create comparative issues.

CHAPTER TWO

PARENTS' WORK ON YOUNGSTERS' EMOTIONAL WELL-BEING

Parents can work on their youngsters' emotional well-being in the following ways:

1. Establish a steady and sustaining climate: Cultivate a climate where your kid has a solid sense of reassurance, cherished, and upheld. Offer predictable profound help and encouraging feedback to assist with building their confidence and strength.

Instructions to assist a kid with building confidence

Encourage kids to have a decent outlook: This is pivotal to emotional well-being. Stress and pessimistic considerations can hinder them and hold them back from feeling their best. Self-uncertainty can be especially troublesome. The accompanying activities can assist with calming internal pundits and mitigate their concerns. As a parent, if you discover your kid stressing as well as naturally suspecting adversely over himself, ask him a few inquiries. For instance: "Is this thought kind to yourself?" "Would you express this to another person?" The responses to these inquiries can frequently assist with diminishing self-questions.

Help your kid to change a negative idea to make it more genuine: For instance, your kid can say something like this: "I get nothing right." Help him to make this more honest by saying all things being equal: "Some of the time you don't get things right, yet different times you do truly extraordinary work. It is alright that you can't do everything, however be pleased with what you can do." You might not have command over what jumps into your brain, however, you truly do have command over what you can zero in on.

Teach your kid self-certification: Help him to remember his value by saying or recording things that he likes about himself. You can also assist him to write them down. When kids regularly recognize the traits they love about themselves, it can give them a tremendous lift in confidence.

2. Energize open correspondence: Make an open and non-critical space for your kid to offer their viewpoints and feelings. Urge them to discuss their sentiments and effectively pay attention to them without excusing or limiting their encounters.

3. Instruct and demonstrate solid adapting abilities: Assist your kid with creating sound survival techniques to oversee pressure and feelings. Model and show procedures like profound breathing, care, active work, and critical thinking techniques. Teach careful contemplation. Careful contemplation is a reflection that expects you to zero in on the current second. Rehearsing careful contemplation puts the center around just being and not doing anything more right now. You can reflect for just 20 minutes out of every day. Indeed, even this sum produces gainful changes in conduct and mind capability. Care diminishes close-to-home reactivity, tension, and depression.

Let your kid eat well: Legitimate eating routines and dietary patterns can likewise help decrease pressure. Eating times should be a quiet, loosened-up experience. Eating should not be done in a hurry. Also, food should not be a system for coping with pressure. A few food varieties contain supplements that assist the body with overseeing pressure. In particular, avocados, bananas, tea, entire grains, greasy fish, carrots, nuts, yogurt, and chocolate are completely remembered to help oversee stress.

Let your kid get sufficient rest: Rest is a period for the body to fix and handle the pressure from the day. It is the time the mind needs to loosen up. It additionally permits the body to loosen up subsequent to utilizing tense muscles over the course of the day. Rest goes about as the reset button for anxiety. It assists with staying away from serious pressure reactions. Kids should get sufficient rest and the rest should be of good quality. Children between the ages of 6 and 13 need around 9 to 11 hours of sleep every night

4. Lay out schedules and design: Reliable schedules assist with giving dependability and a feeling of consistency for kids. Guarantee they have normal rest designs, good dieting propensities, and dispensed time for exercises, homework, and diversion.

5. Energize actual work: Customary activity and actual work have been connected to work on psychological wellness. Urge your kid to take part in age-proper proactive tasks, whether it's playing sports, moving, trekking, or just taking strolls.

6. Give solid outlets to self-articulation: Support inventiveness and self-articulation through exercises like drawing, composing, music, or some other type of craftsmanship that your youngster appreciates. This can give a close-to-home outlet and a feeling of achievement.

7. Limit screen time and screen online exercises: Unnecessary screen time and openness to unseemly substances can adversely influence a kid's emotional well-being. Put forth fitting lines on screen time and screen their internet-based exercises to guarantee their prosperity.

8. Cultivate social associations: Urge your youngster to construct and keep up with solid associations with peers, relatives, and tutors. Support their cooperation in friendly exercises, clubs, or leisure activities where they can communicate with other people who share their inclinations. Social help is significant during troublesome times. Companions, family, and colleagues can all offer consistent reassurance and help with distressing life-altering situations. Social help likewise offers a spot to feel acknowledged and secure.

These parts should be noted in associations

Trust: Trust is vital for building areas of strength for a relationship. It takes into consideration weakness through the private revelation of our most genuine selves.

Regards. Regard in connections implies that you acknowledge the other individual's viewpoints, requirements, and limits. Regard likewise incorporates staying away from pernicious remarks, verbally abusing, and belittling.

Tuning in: Listening is one approach to imparting regard and care to the next individual. Practice undivided attention by permitting a lot of time for the other individual to talk. Observe what they are talking about as well as how they are saying it. Search for others to do the same.

Opportunity: Opportunity in a relationship implies that you permit the other individual time for himself or herself. You additionally permit them to encourage different connections throughout everyday life. It implies that you permit each other to communicate your necessities without consequences

Perceive the elements of unfortunate connections: Sadly, a few connections can be unfortunate or even harmful. Maltreatment in connections is many times about controlling the other individual either genuinely or inwardly. Here are a few ways of behaving that could propose the other individual is harmful:

- Deliberate humiliation
- Being excessively basic
- Disregard
- Being touchy and erratic frequently
- Controlling and restricting other helpful connections
- Utilizing cash to control
- Being possessive
- Showing temper or outrageous desire

Check your kid's circle of friends: Be sure there are no oppressive connections in his day-to-day existence, and consider standing up to the harmful people associated with your kids. Let your kid take part in sound relationship ways of behaving. Keeping up with positive connections isn't just about the ways of behaving of others; it is about one's ways of behaving too. Here are a few ways to keep up with solid relationships:

- Express your requirements and be responsive to the necessities of others.

- Perceive that you won't track down total joy through one relationship.

- Be available to think twice about figuring out how to arrange results you can both acknowledge.

- Acknowledge and adore the distinctions among yourself as well as other people.

- Practice sympathy by attempting to grasp others' insights and perspectives. At the point when difficult issues come up, attempt to haggle with genuineness and empathy.

9. Show critical thinking and flexibility: Assist your youngster with creating critical thinking abilities and the capacity to quickly return from mishaps. Urge them to gain from disappointments, put forth reasonable objectives, and track down ways of defeating difficulties.

Adapting areas of strength can be hard; however, managing them is a piece of participating throughout everyday life. Having the option to manage inclination and mitigate aggravation is a fundamental piece of mental health. A piece of this requires some investment consistently to do things that cause you to feel good.

What encourages children differs. Help your kids identify things that encourage them. Such could be conversing with a companion, going for a stroll, paying attention to music, or participating in another calming movement like an air pocket shower.

Teach your kid to practice mindfulness: Being aware of close-to-home reactions to outside occasions and getting some margin to ponder on responses to troublesome situations is very essential. Rather than responding quickly to a pessimistic occasion, attempts should be made intellectually briefly to take note of close-to-home reactions. Many individuals think that it is useful, for instance, to take two or three full breaths, or build up to ten preceding responding. Ponder feelings without judgment. Doing this permits the space to respond in a manner that isn't imprudent, yet that is smart.

Teaching kids to monitor their feelings is particularly useful in exploring correspondence and connections. Also, teach your kid to keep a diary. Journaling can assist with sorting out viewpoints and sentiments. This can build attention to personal profound responses. It has both mental and actual advantages. Here are some useful diary prompts:

How are my sentiments associated with this occasion?

What do these sentiments inform me concerning myself?

Am I passing judgment on my profound reaction?

What presumptions am I making through my decisions?

Let your kid write in the diary for somewhere around 10 minutes every day.

10. Look for proficient assistance when required: Assuming you notice constant and concerning indications of emotional wellness issues in your kid make sure to provide proficient assistance. Psychological well-being proficiency can give a precise finding and foster a proper treatment plan custom-made to your kid's requirement.

CHAPTER THREE

PERCEIVING PESSIMISTIC SENTIMENTS IN KIDS AND HOW TO HELP

Perceiving pessimistic sentiments in kids is significant as it permits us to offer them backing and train them in sound ways of adapting to their feelings. Here are a few steps you can take to perceive and answer gloomy sentiments in kids in a sound way:

1. Notice and tune in: Focus on changes in your youngster's way of behaving, non-verbal communication, and manner of speaking. They might show indications of trouble, outrage, dissatisfaction, dread, or withdrawal. Pay attention to their words and attempt to comprehend what they are communicating.

2. Establish a protected climate: Give a quiet and supporting climate where your youngster feels open to communicating their feelings unafraid of judgment or discipline. Tell them that it is alright to feel and communicate their sentiments.

3. Approve their feelings: Recognize your kid's sentiments, telling them that encountering a scope of emotions is ordinary. Assist them with putting a name to their sentiments, for example, "I can see that you are feeling upset at the present time." This approval assists them with feeling appreciated and comprehended.

4. Be an attentive person: Show veritable interest and listen mindfully when your youngster shares their feelings. Offer them your full consideration, keep in touch, and give steady non-verbal signs. This sends the message that their sentiments mean a lot to you.

5. Try not to excuse or limit their sentiments: Keep away from phrases like "You're not kidding" and "It's anything but no joking matter." All things considered, understand and attempt to see what is happening according to their viewpoint. Guarantee them that their sentiments are substantial, regardless of whether their response might appear to be unbalanced to you.

6. Show adapting abilities: Assist your youngster with creating solid ways of dealing with their pessimistic feelings. This can incorporate profound breathing activities, discussing their sentiments, rehearsing critical thinking abilities, participating in proactive tasks, or participating in imaginative outlets like drawing or composing.

7. Offer solace and consolation: Show sympathy and deal solace by embracing, nestling, or actual touch assuming your kid is all right with it. Guarantee them that you are there to help them and that encountering troublesome emotions is OK.

8. Energize open correspondence: Make a space where your kid feels happy with examining their feelings with you. Routinely check in with them to perceive how they are feeling and propositions, open doors for them to communicate any worries or stresses.

9. Look for proficient assistance if necessary: In the event that your kid's gloomy sentiments persevere, essentially influence their day-to-day work, or on the other hand assuming you notice concerning ways of behaving, it could be useful to look for direction from a pediatrician, specialist, or school guide.

How to assist kids with overseeing awkward and testing circumstances

To assist kids with overseeing awkward and testing circumstances, you can make the accompanying strides:

1. Keep cool-headed and model flexibility: Youngsters frequently seek their parental figures for direction on the best way to deal with tough spots. Keeping quiet and made can assist with consoling them so that they can defeat difficulties.

2. Support open correspondence: Establish a safe and non-critical climate where youngsters feel happy with discussing their sentiments and concerns. Urge them to offer their viewpoints and feelings straightforwardly unafraid of analysis.

3. Approve their sentiments: Letting youngsters in on that their feelings are legitimate and that feeling awkward or tested in specific situations is typical. Recognize their feelings and convey sympathy by making statements like, "I comprehend that this is hard for you" or "Feeling upset right now is OK."

4. Show critical thinking abilities: Assist youngsters with creating critical thinking abilities by empowering them to thoroughly consider various arrangements or ways to deal with the circumstance. Guide them in conceptualizing and assessing possible arrangements, gauging advantages and disadvantages, and taking into account the results of their activities.

5. Offer consolation and backing: Let kids know that you are there for them and will uphold them through difficult circumstances. Console them that they are in good company and that you have faith in their capacity to beat hardships.

6. Show survival methods: Train youngsters in sound ways of dealing with especially difficult times to deal with their feelings and explore testing circumstances. These may incorporate profound breathing activities, participating in proactive tasks, rehearsing care or unwinding procedures, writing in a diary, or looking for help from confided-in grown-ups.

7. Support strength and a development mentality: Assist youngsters with understanding that misfortunes and difficulties are a piece of life, and they can gain and develop from these encounters. Urge them to see disappointments as any open doors for learning and to foster a positive mentality that advances versatility.

8. Give direction and backing: Offer direction and useful help when required, yet in addition give kids the space to learn and explore testing circumstances all alone. Adjusting backing and independence assists them with creating critical thinking abilities and certainty.

9. Look for proficient assistance if fundamental: In the event that a youngster is reliably attempting to oversee testing circumstances or on the other hand, if their prosperity is essentially influenced, it very well might be useful to look for direction from an advisor, guide, or other qualified experts who work in kid improvement and psychological wellness.

Seven-step intend to show youngsters how to deal with their brain:

Stage 1: Distinguish feelings and considerations

Assist youngsters with becoming mindful of their feelings and considerations. Help them to perceive various feelings they experience and distinguish the considerations that go with those feelings. This mindfulness is the establishment for dealing with their brain successfully.

Stage 2: Challenge negative contemplations

Urge kids to challenge negative or pointless considerations by inquiring as to whether these contemplations are precise or on the other hand in the event that there are elective viewpoints. Help them to supplant negative contemplations with additional positive and reasonable ones.

Stage 3: Practice care

Acquaint youngsters with care practices like profound breathing, body filters, or directed symbolism. Train them to focus on the current second without judgment, assisting them with lessening pressure and centering their brain.

Stage 4: Foster positive self-talk

Train youngsters to utilize positive self-talk by supplanting self-basic or negative considerations with positive and engaging proclamations. Urge them to be their own team promoters and help themselves to remember their assets and capacities.

Stage 5: Put forth sensible objectives

Guide youngsters in laying out practical and feasible objectives. Assist them with separating major objectives into more modest, sensible advances, and help them to celebrate progress en route. This encourages a feeling of achievement and increases inspiration.

Stage 6: Energize critical thinking abilities

Help kids in creating critical thinking abilities to actually oversee difficulties. Train them to distinguish the issue, conceptualize potential arrangements, assess every choice, and pick the best game plan. This enables them to assume command over their circumstances.

Stage 7: Practice taking care of oneself

Assist kids with understanding the significance of taking care of themselves for their psychological prosperity. Show them the worth of exercises like activity, legitimate rest, smart dieting, investing energy with friends and family, chasing after side interests, and enjoying reprieves when required.

Supplanting poisonous considerations with positive ones in kids

Keep an idea diary. Keeping a diary is significant so you can note when these negative contemplations appear, under what conditions, and how you respond to them at the time. Frequently, we have become so acclimated with our negative contemplations that they've become "programmed," or constant reflexes. Pausing for a minute to keep the idea in your diary will start to give you the distance you want to change these considerations.

31

At the point when you have a negative thought, record what the idea was. Likewise, note down the thing that was going on when the idea happened. What's happening with you? Who were you with? Where could you have been? Had whatever happened that could have set off this idea?

Note your reactions at the time. How did you respond, think, or say because of this idea?

Find an opportunity to consider these. Ask yourself how unequivocally you trust these considerations about yourself, and how you feel when you experience them.

Note when you are negative toward yourself. Negative considerations can be about others, yet much of the time, they're about us. Negative convictions about ourselves can appear in regrettable self-assessments. These self-assessments can seem to be "ought to" explanations, for example, "I ought to be better at this." They can likewise seem to be negative markings, for example, "I'm a washout" or "I'm lamentable." Negative speculations are additionally normal, for example, "I'm continuously demolishing everything." These considerations recommend that you have assimilated negative convictions about yourself and acknowledge them as fact. Observe in your diary when you experience considerations like this.

At the point when you record them on paper, attempt to give yourself a little space between yourself and the idea. Get on paper "I had the prospect that I was a failure," as opposed to simply rehashing "I'm a washout." This will assist you in coming to understand that these considerations aren't realities.

Distinguish some issue ways of behaving. Negative contemplations, particularly about us, typically bring about bad ways of behaving. As you record your considerations, focus on the ways of behaving that you use to answer them. A few normal pointless ways of behaving include:

Pulling out from friends and family, companions, and social circumstances

Overcompensating (e.g., taking drastic courses of action to make every other person blissful on the grounds that you believe they should acknowledge you)

In any case, disregarding things (e.g., not reading up for a test since you accept you are "moronic" and will flop)

Being detached as opposed to confident (e.g., not voicing your actual contemplations and sentiments in an unmistakable manner)

Inspect your diary. Search for designs in your negative contemplations that uncover center convictions. For instance, in the event that you often see considerations, for example, "I ought to improve at tests" or "Everybody believes I'm a failure," you might have incorporated a negative central conviction about your capacity to perform, for example, "I'm dumb." You are permitting yourself to think in unbending, nonsensical ways about yourself.

These negative central convictions can cause a great deal of harm. Since they run so profoundly, it's vital to grasp them, instead of simply centering on changing the negative considerations themselves. Simply zeroing in on changing negative considerations is a piece like putting a bandaid on a shot injury: it won't address what's at the foundation of the issue.

For instance, assuming you have a center pessimistic conviction that you are "useless," you will probably encounter a ton of pessimistic considerations connected with that conviction, for example, "I'm disgraceful," "I don't merit anybody to cherish me," or "I ought to be a superior individual." You will likewise presumably see negative ways of behaving connected with this conviction, for example, twisting around in reverse to satisfy a companion since where it counts, you accept you're not deserving of having kinship. You want to provoke the conviction to change the considerations and ways of behaving.

Ask yourself a few hard inquiries. Whenever you've been monitoring your contemplations in a tad, find an opportunity to ask yourself what pointless standards, suspicions, and examples you can recognize in your reasoning. Ask yourself inquiries, for example,

What are my guidelines? What do I view as adequate and unsuitable? Are my guidelines for myself not the same as my norms for other people? How? What do I expect of myself in different circumstances? For instance, how would I anticipate that I should be at the point at which I'm at school, working, mingling, and having some good times, and so on? When do I feel the most reckless or self-questioning? In what circumstances am I hardest on myself? When do I anticipate pessimism? What did my family enlighten me regarding principles and what I ought to and shouldn't do? Do I feel uneasiness in certain circumstances more than others?

CHAPTER FOUR

ASSISTING KIDS WITH ADAPTING TO A TERRIFYING WORLD

Our reality can be an unnerving spot. As parents, we stress over our kids growing up when wars, shootings, bombings, and other terrible demonstrations of viciousness appear to happen in a steady progression. Terrifying pictures stream across our televisions, PCs, and telephones continually. We can't help thinking about how to assist jokes with having a good sense of reassurance and how to converse with them about their feelings of dread and disarray while we attempt to deal with our own. Age, character, formative level, and past life encounters impact how youngsters answer unnerving occasions.

Following are a few normal signs that a kid might be battling to adapt to a terrifying occurrence:

Preschool-age Youngsters

Turning out to be bizarrely calm or upset; expanded apprehension about being separated from everyone else or being isolated from guardians/parental figures; anxiety toward murkiness and outsiders; expanded trouble with changes and advances; return to prior ways of behaving, for example, thumb sucking and "child talk"; loss of hunger or indulging; toileting mishaps.

Young Kids

Trouble falling or staying unconscious; bad dreams; actual grievances like cerebral pains or stomach hurt that don't have a clinical reason; conduct changes, for example, ending up being effortlessly disturbed or forceful; tenacity; stresses over security; trouble concentrating; change in grades or scholarly accomplishment; loss of interest in companions.

Youngsters

Feeling discouraged or irredeemable; segregation from loved ones; changes in eating and rest designs; failure to quit discussing the occasion; loss of interest in friendly exercises; turning out to be less dependable and free; actual grumblings or overstated fears of actual issues; critical increment or reduction in active work.

How You Might Help

With time and backing from parents and other believed grown-ups, most youngsters return to having a solid sense of security not long after the occasion. Here are a few different ways that grown-ups can assist kids with adapting:

Tell your kids that you love them and will protect them.

Small kids could require more embraces and snuggling. Delicate words or simply being available is significant for more established youngsters. Since small kids need actual contact during seasons of pressure to restore a feeling of safety, organized games that permit actual touch with different youngsters might be useful. Educators can sort out games like "Ring around the Rosie," "London Scaffold" or "Duck, Duck, Goose" to work with this.

Instructors of center and secondary school understudies can uphold class activities to assist understudies with directing their sensations of vulnerability and outrage into positive options, for example, raising support or blood drives. Make sense of what occurred as precisely as could be expected yet don't offer realistic subtleties or give more data than your kid requests.

Be accessible to talk and address inquiries at home and in the study hall.

Console kids that discuss how they feel are OK. A few youngsters might not have any desire to discuss their sentiments. Offer other options, such as drawing an image or composing a story.

Since we are encircled by the web, television, radio, and virtual entertainment that frequently replay unnerving pictures, small kids some of the time accept that the occasions are occurring again and again. Small kids ought not to be presented to any media inclusion, especially visual media or pictures. Be mindful so as to screen how much your offspring (of all ages) is presented to the inclusion of the occasion and dispose of their admittance to television or online entertainment if important.

Stick to day to day schedules.

A large portion of us track down solace and consolation in consistency. Dinner times, sleep time, schoolwork, playing with companions, and study hall schedules; are significant for youngsters to keep on encountering as "ordinary" when different things in their reality probably won't be. Deal with yourself and deal with your own pressure in solid ways. Get sufficient rest, eat quality dinners, work out, and converse with different grown-ups. It's typical for youngsters to feel and act stressed, frightened, or confused after an unnerving occasion. These ways of behaving could keep going for a couple of days or even half a month. In the event that they don't improve or deteriorate, now is the right time to look for proficient assistance. Specialists and other psychological wellness experts are prepared with an assortment of proof-based medicines to help kids and grown-ups of any age when their feelings of trepidation and stress don't die down with help at home.

Assisting a Youngster with Managing Awkward Feelings

Intellectually steady kids are in charge of their feelings as opposed to permitting their feelings to control them. Kids who know how to control their sentiments can deal with their way of behaving and keep negative contemplations under control. Yet, kids aren't brought into the world with a comprehension of their feelings and they don't intrinsically have any idea how to communicate their sentiments in socially fitting ways. A youngster who doesn't have any idea how to deal with his resentment might display a forceful way of behaving and incessant unexpected eruptions of fury. Essentially, a youngster who doesn't have any idea what to do when he feels miserable may go through hours frowning without help from anyone else.

At the point when youngsters don't comprehend their feelings, they may likewise keep away from anything that feels awkward. For instance, a kid who is truly bashful in friendly circumstances might try not to join another movement since she needs trust in her capacity to endure the uneasiness related to attempting new things. Training children to direct their feelings can diminish a ton of conduct issues. A youngster who comprehends her feelings will likewise be more ready to manage awkward circumstances and she's bound to perform at her pinnacle. With training and practice, children can discover that they can adapt to their sentiments in a solid way.

Show Moral Obligation

While it's smart for youngsters to encounter a wide cluster of feelings, they really should remember they have some command over their sentiments. A kid who had an unpleasant day at school can pick after-school exercises that help her state of mind. What's more, a youngster who is irate about something her sibling canned tracks down ways of quieting herself down.

Show your youngster sentiments and assist her with understanding that serious feelings shouldn't act as a reason to legitimize bad conduct. Feeling furious doesn't give her an option to hit somebody and sensations of pity don't need to prompt sulking around for a really long time.

Showing your kid that she's answerable for her own way of behaving and faulting others for her feelings is not satisfactory. Assuming that your kid hits her sibling and causes it since he made her frantic, right her wording. Make sense of that everybody is responsible for their own sentiments and their own way of behaving. While her sibling might have impacted her way of behaving, he didn't cause her to feel anything.

Reminding your youngster that she's not accountable for others' emotions is similarly significant. Assuming that she pursues a sound decision, and another person ends up being furious, that is Fine. A significant illustration kids should be built up all through their lives, so they can oppose peer tension and pursue sound choices for themselves. Imparting great qualities and being a solid person will empower your kid to use sound judgment, in spite of others' objections.

Work on Enduring Awkward Feelings

Awkward feelings frequently fill a need. On the off chance for success that you're having on the edge of a bluff, tension is a typical profound reaction that is intended to make us aware of risk. However, here and there we experience dread and tension superfluously.

Show your kid that since she has an anxious outlook on something, doesn't be guaranteed to mean it's an impractical notion. For instance, assuming she's hesitant to join the soccer group since she's anxious she won't have the foggiest idea about any of the different children, urge her to play in any case. Confronting her feelings of trepidation when it's protected to do so will help her see she's prepared to do more than she suspects.

Now and again kids become so used to staying away from the distress that they start to lose trust in themselves. They think, "I would never do that, it'd be excessively frightening." Subsequently, they pass up a great deal of chances throughout everyday life. Delicately push your youngster to step outside her usual range of familiarity. Acclaim her endeavors and clarify that you care more about her eagerness to attempt, as opposed to the result. Show her how to utilize mix-ups, disappointment, and awkward circumstances as any open doors to learn and develop better.

Effective methods to assist with changing a Youngster's Negative State of mind

Youngsters' states of mind are in many cases profoundly reliant upon outer conditions. A kid might be cheerful while she's playing and miserable minutes some other time when now is the ideal time to leave. Then, at that point, her temperament may rapidly move to energy when she learns she'll stop for frozen yogurt coming back. Show your kid that her mindset doesn't need to rely totally upon outside conditions. All things considered, she can have some command over how she feels, no matter what. Enable your kid to do whatever it takes to work on her temperament. That doesn't mean she needs to smother her feelings or overlook them, yet it implies she can do whatever it takes to assist her with feeling quite a bit improved so she doesn't stall out feeling terrible. Moping, confining self, or griping for quite a long time will just keep her inclination terrible. Assist your kid with recognizing decisions she can make to quiet herself down when she's irate or encourage herself while she's inclined to be awful. Distinguish explicit exercises that can help her mindset. While shading might assist one kid with quieting down, another kid might profit from playing outside to consume energy.

Distinguish explicit decisions your kid can make while her inclination is terrible and urge her to work on attempting to assist herself with feeling improved. At the point when you discover her sulking, for instance, take a stab at saying, "I think sulking around today might make you stay trapped feeling terrible. I can't help thinking about how you might help your state of mind?" Empowering your kid to get dynamic or accomplish something else will enable your kid to assume command over her feelings in a solid way.

CONCLUSION

It is critical to recollect that emotional wellness conditions in youngsters are mind-boggling, and their causes can change. Factors like hereditary qualities, cerebrum science, family ancestry, natural stressors, and youth encounters can add to the advancement of these circumstances. If guardians, parental figures, or educators suspect that a youngster might be encountering an emotional well-being condition, looking for proficient assistance from a certified medical care supplier or emotional wellness specialist is urgent. They can lead a careful evaluation, give a precise finding, and make an individualized treatment plan that might incorporate treatments, meds, and backing from the kid's current circumstance.

Early intercession and support can altogether further develop results for youngsters with psychological wellness conditions, permitting them to flourish and lead satisfying lives. It's memorable and vital that every youngster is special and the reasons for emotional wellness issues can change for each person. Looking for proficient assistance can help with understanding and resolving these issues.

www.ingramcontent.com/pod-product-compliance
Lightning Source LLC
Chambersburg PA
CBHW070735260726

48660CB00007B/2865